Anachoresis

Valerie Livina

Contents

EACH TIME WHEN I ATTEMPT TO WRITE ANEW

Each time when I attempt to write anew,
I face familiar frightening dependence:
I feel again as if I never knew
How to create a simple rhymed sentence.

I start with one, and then another word,
Awaiting something that could help expressing
The elusive unformulated thought
That calls for realising and caressing.

Constructing lines, replacing, swapping them,
I'm trying to create a smoothed flow.
I'm working hard; and when it comes to end,
The thought is born, and words begin to glow.

Yet, when it's finished, I am again in doubt:
What if I'll be unable to shape another thought?

HEROISM

I've seen the sites of many battles
And graves without names;
The heroism that shocks and humbles,
The stories that amaze.

I've heard of sufferings so dire:
One soldier stripped of skin,
Another calling own fire
To the place with him within.

A catapulted pilot fell,
Was cornered and shot –
And blew himself, just not to tell
The info that he got.

My heart is mourning every death
On each of fighting sides,
How young and bright they were, how brave,
How short were their lives.

Why do we fight in senseless wars,
Why do we lose the best
In the pursuit to pass resources
To the surviving rest?

We later won't remember cause
Or reasons for the fight,
Yet heroism surpasses wars
And lives beyond their plight.

I'M FIFTY

I'm fifty, yet I feel the same
As 35 or even 13 -
Surprised with every coming day,
Retaining what can't be forgotten.

I'm fifty, as so many were,
And yet will be, among the humans,
I only seek what I adore
I only say what can improve us.

I'm fifty, and I see declines
Of skin and bones, with moods and worries:
What was amusing, now tires;
What was desired, now bores.

I'm fifty, yet I do the splits
And dive a pool of twenty metres
My ageing body still resists
To stop proceed, however dithers.

I'm fifty, soon I will be gone,
Without sadness or self-pity;
Another poet will be born,
More skilful and perhaps more witty.

I'm fifty, and I'm still the soul
That seeks adventure and attachment -
Curiosity that isn't worn,
And passion of the finest parchment.

WHEN ELDERS LEAVE

When elders leave, and we become the elders
In separation that we cannot mend;
When elders leave, we're left as new defenders
Of values they have passed us to defend;

When elders leave, remember their faces,
As no excuse will be accepted since,
No chance to meet, - just serve your painful sentence
And pray for the forgiveness of the sins.

NORWICH CATHEDRAL

I'm coming every week
To stop being weak,
To charge my faith
And to be able to think and to create.

I CAME TO LIFE WITH MANY QUESTIONS

I came to life with many questions;
For answers, I was given voice:
To know the world - with no possessions,
And to adore - with no response.

THE FORCE THAT'S GIVEN FOR TODAY

The force that's given for today -
Do spend it all, without idleness,
Do sing the melody of God
In human voice; don't stay in silence!

I DON'T WANT FAME

I don't want fame, it is an ugly creature:
It chooses blindly, stupidly avoids.
Yet neither pure luck, nor grand achievements,
Too early to pretend for fruitful joys.

The fame is vain, it passes very quickly,
By silly caprice it ignored Bach!
He was unknown - just to live forever,
And famous ones are all forgotten dust.

No, I don't want that fame, I want my path,
I want to find the words that sound forte,
I want to fire the candle by strength of love,
Not silly fame - I want to be immortal!

WESTMINSTER ABBEY

The Latin prints on famous graves:
The kings, the nobles, the knights, the clergy -
They all obtained final peace
Within the walls of ancient Abbey.

This one was smart, that one was brave,
The sly, the prosperous, the lucky:
So famous names, so noted lives
The best imprints of human nature.

I walk along on scared legs:
I am ashamed that I'm above you,
You gathered here to remind
About vanity of living.

Near the exit, lays a grave -
It's very simple, no bust or statue
No even name, just plain words,
They move and make one to remember:

"He had been found overseas,
His name's unknown, yet immortal,
He gave his life for all the dear -
He died for God, for King and country."

And all the glory of the kings
Is shadowed by this engraving;
Such death equated him to them,
And even higher elevated.

I stay in tears - tears of delight:
His death was neither long, nor painful,
The noble death of young and brave -
This is the true and final Glory.

MY BICYCLE

My bicycle's fast,
My bicycle's cool
I manage to press,
I manage to roll.

It's better than car,
It's faster than walk,
It's clean, it's fun
It's smooth - it's my bike!

I now ride fast,
Then slow I ride
Then jump as a blast -
My bike is my pride!

Yeah, biking is flying,
Yeah, biking is cool.
Who thinks that I am lying
Is certainly a mule.

I see a policeman,
I send him regards:
No number, no licence -
I am free, and I am nuts!

He won't ever stop me,
He won't ever fine
The rules aren't for bikers -
Yeah, biking is fun!

I'm fast as two trams
Or as half of a taxi!
No crowds, no gas -
And freedom at maxi!

I skip the hitchhikers:
Too busy to stop;
I'm hacker of roads,
Not scared of cops.

Pedestrian, drivers,
Go now to stores,
Convert into bikers -
All transport is worse!

I ADD TWO PEARLS TO MY BIZZARE COLLECTION

I add two pearls to my bizarre collection -
It's neither rich, nor vast, although priceless,
It has comprised some words and rare glances -
My only treasure, my divine resource.

One pearl - that glance, so sharp and unexpected,
Yet full of open and naive intention
To know sooner, closely and completely;
There's no better jewel than the glance.

Another pearl - the moment at departure,
The gustiness instead of silly speeches,
Most pleasant and exciting impoliteness:
The secret is no secret anymore.

In four long years, fondest of besiegement
Has brought its fruits; I bundle them in the words.

HOW POETRY IS DIFFERENT FROM PROSE?

How poetry is different from prose
Isn't easy to deduce in modern writings:
No rhymes, no rhythm, excessively verbose,
And sense is either missing or departing.

Some earlier relaxed rules of genre
And opened Pandora's box with flooders -
Artistic profanation had began,
And poetry abuse then reached its rudest.

How can I fit contemporary art?
I am a stranger, lacking sense of modern:
I want my poetry to have what I regard
As two most quintessential components.

There should be music blended with idea -
That is the real poetry's ideal.

SCIENCE CLAIMS THAT LOVE IS A STRAIGHTFORWARD ACT

Science claims that love is a straightforward act
Of genes and biochemical reactions.
What puzzles me - all theories intact -
The curious enigma of attraction.

It brings together birds to build a nest,
(In hope for pleasures and that genes passing?)
Do humans have such basic interests,
Or something rather grander and surpassing?

I want to be with you because of genes?
Of chemistry? Of the unlikely offspring?
In our union, do the instincts win
Because of some molecules in the nostrils?

In search for mechanisms, science lost its truthful path...
To be complete - that's why I need your love!

MONTAIGNE

Montaigne was born in fifteen thirty three;
Yet when I read his so back-dated writings,
They are as new and fresh in their decree
As if he were my pal in nineteen nineties.

He helped me navigate the troubled times,
When little world of mine was shuttered and ruined,
When I was pushed to learn, to live and rhyme,
And find the balance of restrain and doing.

He is as modern and as versatile
As those .Greek stoics that he chose as teachers -
No matter how the society declines,
Such giants appear among the sinful creatures.

I work towards the same sincere goal:
To understand the major human role.

MORAL OUTCASTS

I read that yachts belong to "moral outcasts",
Which sounds well and makes one feel above them;
Those people's riches are unfair and vast,
And come with amorality in tandem.

To wish to build a business is a gift,
Constructive and respectable endeavour;
When it's successful, and the goal's achieved,
That's a fulfilling stage of proper level.

Yet, when the money comes with this success,
Who would then waste it for the mindless symbols?
That kind of people do, indeed, transgress
Morality domain in their wellness.

When money's come, it's time for "good" and "must",
Otherwise, one does become a moral outcast.

MEDIOCRITY

When mediocrity obtains the full control
Of arts and crafts, opinions and morale,
And dominates all media to troll
Those who lose pace in this unequal rally,

It then supports the victory of sins
As deviation from the common greyness:
When good is boring, evil starts to seem
Acceptable for many of the brainless.

There is no tool to terminate the stream
Of the degrading mediocre production;
They praise each other, riding for esteem
And ruin others in arranged reaction.

A single talent can't resist the bunch -
It disappears, unknown and detached.

SPECTACULAR COLLAPSE OF STATES AND WALLS

Spectacular collapse of states and walls
May seem abrupt and even entertaining:
They helped achieve the democratic goals,
Created new elites in fortunes gaining.

But do you think of those who lived at roots
And underwent prolonged collapse and chaos?
They didn't get capitalistic fruits -
Instead, they got just wars and empty vows.

Did you expect those huge misplaced groups?
Did you anticipate the brutal conflicts?
Did you just hope to solve them, sending troops?
Are you, at least, ashamed of your involvement?

And even now, thirty years passed,
It's still bloodshed and struggle, unsettled dust...

IN SEARCH FOR LOVE

In search for love, we spend those many years
In doubts and hopes, uncertain all the way:
If love exists, then how it appears,
And if it doesn't, why live another day?

Then after many bitter disappointments,
It does arrive and maintains its sway;
When separated, time is stopped by longing,
And when together, time just melts away.

Then years start to vanish ever faster,
And leave so ever shorter time for us;
Not having centuries for love is a disaster,
While learning slow, we expire fast...

When one finds love, remaining time is short;
For every day, be grateful to your lord.

THE MODERN STATES

The modern states aren't solid anymore,
They cannot make a unified effort.
They are concerned with riches; therefore
Betraying everything that they were set for.

The more diverse, the smaller common base,
The more alienated social stratas,
The worse the economical disgrace,
The sparser the communal human lattice.

Two main subgroups, the powerful and not,
Stand in positions on unequal grounds:
Those who can live wherever's money pot,
And those who have their roots in local mounds.

The fight isn't equal, yet in our lands
There are still strong and patriotic lads.

AS I LOOK BACK AT MANY PAST EVENTS

As I look back at many past events,
It seems that I was born to be a poet:
Among the books, worshipping word and sense,
Yet poor, yet not needy, yet not worried.

Without understanding cost of things,
Without urge to hold the once obtained,
Not trained to admire what riches bring,
And not inclined to any kind of gaining.

Through education, travel, need to work,
I have been forced to the sole goal:
Refining writing skills around the clock,
To formulate the beauty as a whole.

Since early days, I live to say these lines,
Ensuring beauty never fades or declines.

PSYCHOLOGY ATTEMPTS TO TREAT DISTRESS

Psychology attempts to treat distress
And promises some cures for distressed:
Discussions recommended for obsessed,
And exercise for violent and restless.

But stress has always been a sign of move,
Accompanying efforts and achievements;
Why would one want the stress to be removed?
Would it improve our sense of self-fulfilment?

We have to maintain the inner core,
Integrity of "stiffer-upper-lippers" -
That'll help us to survive and to restore
The balance that's unknown for the weepers.

At every plane of this mundane existence,
Choose right behaviour and level of persistence.

WHEN SCHUBERT PAID FOR DINNERS WITH HIS SONGS

When Schubert paid for dinner with his songs,
He couldn't imagine times of modern music,
Where Eminem and Britney Spears belong
To pantheons of giants, with past refused.

Electric wonders bring us other rhythms
And mask the clear lack of a genuine talent,
If one considers the music underneath,
It is devoid of quality and barren.

Like science, new music grows ever large,
With millions earned by very simple inventions.
Consumerism supports its noisy march,
Its primitive and mercantile intentions.

When money dominates the world of art,
Expect not quality but cultural hazard.

TWO GENTLEMENT DISCUSS THE HEATHROW NEWS

Two gentlemen discuss the Heathrow news
And ponder how expansion will be going.
They blame the government for budgeting abuse
And disapprove unnecessary growing.

They are in their 80s, and as such
Are both unlikely to observe the changes,
Yet, they're concerned and complaining much:
Good citizens, disliking chains and cages.

They think ahead, planning for decades,
Although their own lives will finish sooner,
They operate remote and abstract dates,
Forgetting death in their world sublunar.

It's good to think and plan beyond our lives,
So that society continues and survives.

CONCEPTUAL ART

The name "conceptual" is given to the art
That has ambition of becoming mainstream;
Its lack of skill is an important part
Of the communal sinecural nesting.

One lack of talent helps another lack
By praising similarities in "lackness";
They keep each other on career track
In academic teaching and pedantness.

They squeeze away all other types of art
And form sick tastes and perverse opinions.
They substitute by evil every part
That should promote civility and brilliance.

They are malign, they're harmful for the taste;
The real art just suffers, being displaced.

I AM A STRANGER

I am a stranger stuck between two shores:
Forever alien, one way or another:
What one of countries worships and adores
Is hated and despised by the other.

The weirdest thing is that they are the same:
Imperial, robust, heroic nations,
They trace their roots from prehistoric days
And find the same solutions and inventions.

In their equal powers and prides,
They keep competing, as they strive for glory -
To one another, each of them denies
Objective picture or a balanced story.

I love them both; in each I stay alone:
While speaking truth, misjudged, attacked, and worn.

WE HAVE TO CLIMB

We have to climb in order to avoid
The surely upcoming degradation:
The years unavoidably embroider
Our wrinkled faces and confused actions.

When yet another effort brings success,
It is postponing end, but not denying.
No need for any educated guess:
I know what is ahead lying.

To those who die in their own bed,
With families and peaceful preparations,
I tell that I prefer a sudden end,
While swimming, jumping, cycling - full of action.

To go with open eyes and breathing chest -
Without help of busy NHS.

MY FAITH IS SIMPLE

My faith is simple, as simple is my belief
In living plain, avoiding complications.
I pray one God, in happiness and grief,
Without sentimental exaltation.

I see that power in every little thing,
It penetrates the space and single moments,
It gives me proper strength and will to think
(Sometimes, it helps somebody fly to a comet.)

This faith unites for me the whole world
As an enormous dedicated vessel,
I see the true religious stronghold
In all religions where there is that blessing.

My faith is simple; I pray the only God
As the combining, unifying global node.

I WISH I WOULD BE GONE

I wish I would be gone well in advance
Before the world explodes in sheer madness:
It is developing towards a smaller chance
Of the survival on the brink of vengeance.

Unrest and greed, possessiveness and lust,
All drive us packed in the same direction.
The modern world without peace or trust,
Or a hope for kindness, taste, or gentle affection.

Sustainability of growth serves as a myth
Before the dreamt stability achieved:
The human race has rotted underneath,
And quality - by numbers outlived.

We head a crash; no way to slow the pace,
It will reshape again the human race.

I STILL CAN TRAVEL

I still can travel any given moment,
A light backpack would serve my humble needs;
Today I pack it and tomorrow drop it,
Agile and ready for required deeds.

I am unsettled, with uncertain future,
Which was somehow a goal in the past.
Life has provided me with basic nurture,
I can't complain; I'm doing what I must.

Security, or wealth, or a steady venue
Are not my blessing; life is often rough.
I live in prayer, trying to continue, -
And if I can't, I rise to change my path.

I will re-settle among new fields and brooks,
Although it's sad to leave behind old books.

TO KNOW IT ALL

To know it all, exalting or disgusting,
We learn from artists of all kinds and sorts.
Curiosity appears ever-lasting
And may be our finishing resort.

To learn about new unknown creatures,
New cultures from obscure unknown lands,
Or recognise details of known features
And of familiar or spooky foreign strands.

This world of the established entertainment
Create all products, plenty and abound;
The genres are formatted, trimmed, framed, -
Just follow others and complete your happy round.

But closer human truth would never sell:
Demand is nil, as markets know well.

NEW TRENDS

New trends declare equality in arts:
Just start "creating" and become an artist!
Would one attempt such silliness in maths?
You try it, and will see your work in tatters.

One can achieve the heights in only way:
A born-in talent, years of skill-building.
All other ways would lead a soul astray:
Lies and ambitions, polished and gilded.

Not everyone is destined to achieve -
No matter how equality is claimed.
That only makes the common level cheap,
And only kitsch and spam can be obtained.

"Equality" helps mediocre to thrive -
And makes impossible for talents to survive.

THE PROMISE OF A SOUL

"The promise of a soul that's good for me"
Is the defining feature of attraction;
It may be brutal or strangely feminine,
Depending on the object, time and action.

We look into a face and see the soul,
And may it be a beauty or a cripple,
Its features bring emotions to recall -
All kinds of faces for all kinds of people.

And why the need to seek another half?
I don't accept those silly explanations
Of gene exchanges on the group's behalf:
Love is much higher than a basic function.

I love because it makes me feel complete:
"The useful soul" has come to heal our split.

I SEE SOME OLDER PEOPLE

I see some older people - lonesome, sad -
Whose brains descend into a mental illness;
Their personalities become untimely cut,
And death arrives before the body weakens.

We, humans, now live much longer lives,
Of which the most we spend routinely working;
Between the boring duties, we disguise
Our dreams that we're perpetually blocking.

And then comes freedom, when there is no health,
To leave one face the hypothetic options:
Will one enjoy the hard-obtained wealth,
Or sleep with no ideas or emotions?

I don't want live until the gruesome age,
When one becomes apathic and estranged.

WHEN FEELINGS ARE INTENSE

When feelings are intense and cause your pain,
When every move is filled with emotions,
When those emotions muddle your every day,
And you are hurt each time without a caution;

When you attempt transform that into art,
When art becomes the only route to freedom,
When it releases something dark and hard,
Yet, puts your soul into a calmer kingdom;

When you've expressed what called to be expressed,
When this releases the sickening obsession,
When written lines remove that painful stress
And bring detachment from remaining passions;

Enjoy some time without need to write -
It will return tomorrow, burning bright.

IN THE BEGINNING

In the beginning, nothing's clear,
All possibilities are vague;
You try to find the right career,
Ask for advice, or even beg.

Then, forced by the circumstances,
You start to follow a single path,
You learn a craft and use the chances
To progress in artistic love.

Priorities become apparent,
Side-lining pleasure or caprisse,
And skills, being furthered by the talent,
Produce a lasting masterpiece.

It takes all life and can't be stopped;
Embrace its force and learn to cope with.

I'M BETTER WHEN I WRITE

I'm better when I write; this helps exceed
The basic level of mundane existence.
It hurts to live; the pain induces need
To sooner pass the current living instance.

I climb and fight, without wanting much;
I do my duties, year after year,
I try to stay as balanced and detached,
As useful and engaged as I can bear.

I see the end before the others start;
I feel too tired to enjoy the process;
My mind was old before I would grow-up,
And knew the pain before the coming losses.

It is the Saturn, punisher and teacher,
Who drags me, to improve the sinful creature...

SICK ARTISTS

Sick artists keep creating sinful art,
Sick critics keep appraising their sickness;
They tear the real art and gifts apart
Possessing neither patience nor meekness.

How can one better represent true love
Than by a goat piercing tractor tyres?
What looks plain ugly has been praised above
The "boring" classics, - and the art expires.

That's why their common genres of preference
Are tricks, satire, porn and provocations;
No real creativity in thence;
They ride the wave of basic crude attractions.

High style requires skills and public culture;
Without those, arts heads for departure.

EARTH, MOON AND SUN

Earth, Moon and Sun, aligned for eclipse,
Look as a random meaningless arrangement:
As random as the planetary bliss
Of life on Earth, with species, tribes and legends.

We have been told: it's all about chance,
With probabilities as little as non-existent;
Yet, it appeared in galactic dance,
And flourished despite the vast resistance.

And those three bodies, different in size,
Obedient to the non-ending practice,
Align for us in their perfect stance,
To awe and fascinate us through the darkness.

If an eclipse is not a sign of God,
What else can show that atheism is flawed?

THE GLIMPSE OF HISTORY

The glimpse of history is visible today
In shared roots and similar expressions:
The common past exists in modern days
Of the combined European nations.

The same ideas of the common jokes,
In Padua, in Hamburg and in Bristol;
Londinium is roman in its docks,
And French "bistro" derives from Russian "bystro".

The Latin can be trac'd in Portuguese,
And Russians read French-named "belletristics";
"Stuck" and "anzatz" are German modest lease,
And Greeks originated chrematistics.

We are so close in our common home;
In Swedish - "hem", in Russian - also "dom".

POLITICS

When politics appears in the arts,
It is an easy way to grab attention
That turns the heroes into comic nuts —
Here comes the well-deserved gratification.

Make people laugh at simple and easy jokes,
Make villains vile, according expectations,
Make the consumers of your art enjoy
The pictures of expectable relations.

That kind of art is not a rocket science,
It is paid well, it brings artistic laurels,
Whether or not it may survive the times,
It brings to life some entertaining colours.

Alas, I cannot do that kind of art,
Being born as a lamenting sorrowful bard.

BAD ART

There is no question: what is made is art;
The question is: how good its level should be
To be deserving even a tiny part
Of our time on Earth, consumed shrewdly?

While some of them pretend to entertain,
And others puzzle by non-existent substance,
The most of them just fail to maintain
Aesthetic skills required of masters.

A lot of art, despite reviews, is bad;
Conceived by drive for honours, fame and money;
No praise of critics is amending that,
However hard they may be truth denying.

Let any art exist, but learn to know
Which one is placed high and which is low.

THE HUMAN ANIMAL

The human animal will ever live in a body,
That has its basic needs and sinful joys.
Its fight with soul, permanent and bloody,
Will never stop, being tortured by choice.

Whether excess or pious abstention,
Both ends deny a soul short-living peace,
To choose a path of work and dedication,
Avoid extremes with dangerous abyss.

Then wait for luck that promises some balance,
And peace of mind, and even a humble content,
And then create, avoiding wasteful malice,
Commit your gift in a dutiful attempt.

Then let it be, expecting no redemption,
You had it all in process of creation!

IN A LONG-TERM LOVE

In a long-term love, our bodily decline
Influences emotions and attachment;
Some of its signs are painful and malign
As scratches on fragile perceptive parchment.

This distances the best of loving couples;
They drift away from their early passion;
What was instinct and genuine, now baffles
And makes no sense of their past attraction.

Some other couples continue holding flame,
Which in itself is a subject of amazement.
Those happy few sustain their loving game
That cannot be enforced or purchased.

If you are lucky to be loved like this,
Prolong each night and every tender kiss.

WHEN FEMINISM REQUIRES EQUAL RIGHTS

When feminism requires equal rights,
I wonder how men and women can be equal?
They have achieved equality at nights,
But woman still remains a baby vehicle.

She is unwell when men may call for battles,
However hard she tries, her muscles are weaker,
She well deserves all feminine discounts,
She tires sooner, her attention flickers.

But she creates as well as any man,
And for results, deserves full scale of justice;
She does sometimes much more than what she can,
And stands against the chauvinistic nasties.

Equality exists among the minds,
And those deserve respect and equal rights.

THE WORDS OF LOVE

The words of love cannot compare with science
In profit and impact utilisation,
As science so undeniably combines
Advances of a mature civilization.

The words of love cannot provide defence,
They have no use in building living comforts,
They often bear not much of common sense,
And can't compare with engineering wonders.

The words of love can only help express
The struggle and pain of the pulsating soul -
To paint emotions in their instant mess
Is their ultimate poetic goal.

The words of love can still affect our life:
They have ability - through centuries survive.

I OVERHEARD A CLEAVER CONVERSATION

I overheard a clever conversation
Of elderly respected gentlemen:
They were discussing science, United Nations,
Technologies, invasions, and boheme.

The BBC provided common topics -
I recognised every single thread, -
Their middle-class Britishness was spotless,
It only gets more stiffened under threat.

Then they discussed the pains of immigration,
Complaining of the cultural impact.
As "papists" were dismissed by the nation,
So are the wildlings of the current act.

Through centuries, the people stay the same:
Smart, eloquent, reserved - shine or rain...

IT'S HUNDRED YEARS

It's hundred years since the Russian tsar
Was overthrown in the red uprising,
Since the bloodthirsty communistic star
Began its way, both sinister and dazzling.

As there are always reasons for unrest,
It's utilised by the worst of people:
By careerists with murky interests
And by the sharks who use them as a weapon.

The sharks arrive to steal the nation's trove,
While new elite are ready to repay them -
Thus Lenin was installed for alien growth,
Prepared to withdraw and surrender.

A revolution is an evil dirty act,
Its function is to steal, degrade, destruct.

WHEN LEAVING RUSSIA

When leaving Russia, I had left the ship
That was half-sunk, unsuitable for living;
Unable to save it, I could only weep
And try to find another place for new beginning...

After departure, I observed the change
From rags to riches, in some fifteen years;
It took a leader, efforts and avenge
To wake and nourish the lethargic Russian bear.

Now, prosperous and strengthened by trouble,
The country celebrates its new revival:
Its fairs and churches, full of gold and marble,
Are joy for Russians, awe for the rivals.

Although my generation has been lost,
It's good to see that Russia's passed the worst.

YOUR BEAUTY ISN'T WANING

Your beauty isn't waning, never so,
But years make imprint on our faces,
Denoting time as accurate Tissot,
Reminding us: the final end commences.

Not loss of beauty but the loss of love
Is what entrains my poor heart with sadness...
I still may hope for meeting you above,
I'm eager to believe in any chances.

We'll meet again, in a maybe better world,
Where we will have all time to give each other,
Where will be no distraction or discord,
And life will have no obstacles or shadows.

We'll meet again, I know this for certain,
As love like ours can never be forgotten.

PAST, FULL OF ERRORS AND MISTAKES

Past, full of errors and mistakes,
Doesn't go away, and only grows;
The present is an unhappy fake,
The future's a shadow of unknowns.

For all the sins of shameful past,
I beg forgiveness of mistreated;
I recollect it with disgust,
And I am sad that may repeat it.

My sinful shell in painful world
Was dropped to float with no direction;
I've learnt the power of words,
And even that is an imperfection.

I browse my unfulfilling life
And have no willing to survive.

SOMETIMES WE HAVE A MOMENT OF DISCORD

Sometimes we have a moment of discord,
And what we love appears almost alien,
We're ready to accept and take onboard
Suspicions, disappointments and denials.

The stress of life may often overwhelm,
It blows problems out of proportions;
Some doubts may overshadow our gem -
The dedicated love and true emotions.

And then you bring a card with words of peace,
And I bring mine, selected one of dozens,
We open them, and get surprised with this:
They are the same, though separately chosen.

Being so alike is a striking sign of fate -
It cannot be dismissed or betrayed.

WHEN LOVE MATURES

When love matures, escaping routes to failure,
And promises the ever-lasting peace,
When everything settles down, as in favour
Of the complete and perfect home bliss,

How often it is cut by tragic crashes,
By sudden deaths and senseless accidents,
How often our love ends up in ashes
By means of uncontrollable events.

I know this too well to feel rejoiced,
While living as a loved and loving wife,
It's scary how random are the choices,
How very short and how fragile is life.

With thoughts of this, at every happy moment,
I'm frightened of losing my beloved.

IF YOU OBSERVE THE HAPPY CYCLISTS

If you observe the happy cyclists
With silly grins upon their muzzles,
If all the human sins and vices
Look as remote and pointless puzzles,

If you can stop and call in forest
For legendary Lorelei,
And forest, as a perfect florist,
Sends buds and whispers in reply,

If every minute lasts forever,
And you aren't eager to arrive,
Despite the miles and freezing weather,
You feel again as twenty five, -

Without a guide or a noisy group,
You're cycling on the blue Danube!

FAITH WITHOUT A THOUGHT

As faith without a thought is sentimental,
So a thought without faith is mental spam;
A human life, to be fulfilled and gentle,
Requires both - to grow and overcome.

As beauty with no art is too short-living,
So art without beauty is a crime:
Art with no talent cannot be forgiven -
Incapable of a melody or rhyme.

When art is flooded by the evil vendors,
Of poor merit, chasing easy fame,
Scandalousness is their only splendour, -
Uneducated public shares blame.

Thoughts with no faith, as art without beauty
Lead to the culture that is void and looted.

IS A TRAGEDY STILL POSSIBLE TO WRITE?

Is a tragedy still possible to write
In the confusing age of shallow wonders?
When public looks for laughter and delight
And publishers seek poems on footballers?

Does real tragedy continue to exist
When death is either nuisance or statistics?
When talents drift to novelties and twists
And money comes with thicker belletristics?

There may be no updated version of Macbeth,
And Hamlet would end up in a happy marriage -
Those deaths would be so easy to prevent
In modern world; no-one would need to perish.

Under the flood of gossips, news, and lies,
The only tragedy is our wasted lives.

CLIMATE CHANGE

The public interest in climate change
Is most commendable in its intentions,
In giving us a slim survival chance,
And certain hopes for future generations.

Yet, people do not think of dying soils,
Of drinking water that is getting sparser.
That'll trouble us long before the planet boils,
Before we find a living place on marses.

The only way to face the coming age
Is to reduce and circumvent consumption:
For waste and carelessness, the nature will revenge
Much worse than the UN with any sanctions.

Consume what's really needed, no excess,
Avoid the false directions to progress.

CONSPIRACIES

Conspiracies and theories of life
Are an intrinsic side of human nature:
The complex brain is struggling to survive
Its largely hopeless, unproductive venture.

Not all such patterns really exist,
But rather are a product of obsession;
When uncontrolled, mind is a tricking beast,
Quite able of the prolonged self-deception.

Asperger is a plague of modern times,
Confusing, driving mad without cure;
No longer can religion help with vice,
And knowledge builds, which mind cannot endure.

Without principles, abundance and disorder
Result in mindlessness, which only grows broader.

HAYDN

The pleasantness of Haydn can't be disputed,
He is a giant of that refined epoch;
So full of light, melodically rooted,
He's one of finest masters of baroque.

But I would struggle to memorise his pieces,
Despite his talent and produced track:
There is that something that his music misses -
Originality? Uniqueness? Higher spark?

How important is to live with thunders:
To have own voice and a matching vital force.
Nowadays, those are replaced by scandals,
Instead of brightness - splashes of compost.

To have a talent is a rare gift;
To have it bright is a dream to be achieved.

CONFUSED AND UNCERTAIN

Confused and uncertain how to bear it,
Being pushed between too many interests,
I've finally received an advice of merit:
"Do what feels right and throw away the rest".

But what feels right doesn't bring appreciation,
And cannot pay one's daily living bills;
Unable to earn by beauty adoration,
A poet has to build some other skills,

And then to balance art with calls of duty
By means of shorter sleep and longer work.
While body operates, the soul can't be muted,
As breath continues, and the heart tick-tocks.

The need to balance those is good for brain;
Still, art would benefit from smaller strain.

THERE ARE JUST FOUR MAIN TYPES OF ART

There are just four main types of art,
Just two criteria to weigh them;
It's easy then to split apart
Those that are trivial or seldom.

First, if an artist has a gift:
A talent, bright and outstanding:
The one that's broadly perceiv'd
As masterstroke with fortune blended.

Then each of these unequal groups
Divides again by good or evil,
The good's inspired by cherubs,
The other drags your soul to devil.

I want to face the only type:
The gifted good that brings enlightenment.
I would be happy to retire
And live in beautiful confinement.

An artist is a soul guide -
Don't follow those that aren't right.